PERFECT & LOVE

Andrew Murray

GH

www.gideonhousebooks.com

Perfect Love

Andrew Murray

© 2016 Gideon House Books

Published by:
Gideon House Books
2137 Ash Grove Way
Dallas, TX 75228

ISBN-13: 978-1-943133-42-0

Also from Gideon House Books

Missionary Methods: St. Paul's or Ours? by Roland Allen

Humility: The Beauty of Holiness by Andrew Murray

The Essentials of Prayer by E.M. Bounds

Till He Come by C.H. Spurgeon

Sovereign Grace by D.L. Moody

God's Light in Dark Clouds by Theodore Cuyler

A Church in the House by Matthew Henry

Indwelling Sin in Believers by John Owen

Secret Power by D.L. Moody

Thoughts for Young Men by J.C. Ryle

The Divine Liturgy of St. John Chrysostom

A Study on Dispensationalism by A.W. Pink

Prevailing Prayer: What Hinders It by D.L. Moody

The Duty of Pastors by John Owen

The Expulsive Power of a New Affection by Thomas Chalmers

According to Promise by Charles Spurgeon

The Resurrection: A Symposium by Charles Spurgeon

The Acceptable Sacrifice by John Bunyan

Find these titles and more at
www.gideonhousebooks.com

PREFACE

THE two following addresses were delivered, the first at the opening, and the second at the close of the South African Keswick of 1893. They are like those published under the title of "Jesus Himself," a reprint from the *South African Pioneer*, the organ of South African General Mission, of which the Rev. Andrew Murray is president. They are sent out with the hope that they may be, under God, a means of much blessing to many.

14A, *Lingfield Road,*
Wimbledon

PERFECT LOVE

DEAR friends, in the name of our blessed Lord Jesus, I bid you welcome to this our Convention. May the blessing of God Almighty, the Father, the Son and the Holy Ghost rest upon every one of you. We are met in the name of Jesus Christ, that Name which avails in heaven more than thought can think, that Name that has had power in hell to cast out devils, that Name that can bless us beyond all power of thought. We are met in the living Name of the living Jesus. Welcome all, and let us seek with one heart and one mind to take up the posture of prayer in which to ask God to reveal the love that passeth knowledge—

The Perfect Love

we are met to seek. The more I thought of our Convention as it has been coming on, the more I felt how little we know what we are. To think that that Everlasting God who created heaven and earth, should deal with each one of us individually—with *me*, and that it should please Him to take out of the fountain of His everlasting Godhead, and to fill me with that everlasting love in which the Father begot the Son, and in which the Holy Spirit maintains the fellowship between Father and Son.

I want this evening very simply to try and give you some thoughts to open up the subject, by way of preparation for the following days. Let my text be the words that you have as the motto of our Convention:

"God is Love."

You find them twice in the fourth chapter of the first Epistle of John.

"God is Love." What does that mean? Well, I think it means at once and first of all, that I must not seek for love, for I may fail. If I want love I must seek God, for love is the very nature of God. It does not say God *has* love, but God *is* love, and

The Love that I need

is God Himself coming into my heart. We have met together to study this infinite Word of perfect love. Let us begin by saying, "God is Love." Not a drop of pure, real, heavenly, everlasting love can come to us, but God must be moved to give it as an act of His grace.

God has revealed His love in all nature, even in the very animals. Look at the way the little lamb clings to its mother, and the way the mother sheep cares for the lamb. That is what we call love. And so amongst the most savage and most ungodly heathen, you can find love of a certain sort.

But the love of heaven, the love of eternity, that will last, the love that is not in the flesh, but that comes from heaven, that love is God, and if

I Want that Love

I must have God. What a thought! Oh! let us bow in humble praise. I want this great God to come into me and take possession of me, and to make me a vessel fit for His use, that He can fill me with love. Let every heart say: "Yea! my God! take me and fill me with love, for the sake of Thy Son who died on Calvary."

As I said, I just want to give you a few thoughts this evening by way of preparation for the next three days. The first question is, "What do we need? What is it that brought us together? What is it we seek?" Then our second question will be, "What are we to do, what have we to do to get what we are seeking?" And then the third question, "What are we to expect?"

Now first,

What is it we Seek?

Somebody asked me the question two days ago: "What suggested that subject of perfect love for your Conference?" and my answer was very simple: "We felt there was such a need of it." And just look round and think what a need there is. Is not this the one thing in your Christian life? Look first of all at your relationship to God. Do you know the love of God as you ought to know it? Does it dwell upon you as an overshadowing power, the way the love of a mother dwells upon the child that lives in her smile?

Do you know the Love of God,

and does it make you from morning to night sing the song of the ransomed ones? There is not a heart but says: "Oh! I know the love of God too little." And why is that? It is because you have not been perfected in love, because when the soul is perfected in love it has got such a sense of that love that it can rest in it for eternity, and though it has as much as it can contain for the time being it can always receive more. Again, is there no dissatisfaction with your love to God? You sometimes think that you can say: "Oh! my God, I do love Thee." There are many Christians who don't say that—real Christians. They are afraid to say it. They fear God, and they say earnestly: "I wish to love God," and they complain very honestly and bitterly, "Oh! my God,

Why have I so little Love?"

but they hardly know what it is to say, "Oh! thou God of Heaven, how I love Thee! Thou knowest how my heart delights in Thee." What a joy to know that! Oh! have you not had to confess often and often that you could not speak like that to God? And does there not come up in the heart a strong feeling of condemnation? "Alas, my love to God is not what it should be!" And then sometimes when you have a sense of God's love given to you for a moment in your fellowship with God, is there not a cry, "Oh! why can it not abide with me?"

The child has no trouble in rejoicing in its parents' love. I remember my little boy or girl of five or six, sometimes coming to the study door, and opening it, and just looking in and smiling to see papa's face, and then shutting the door and going away happy; or coming on tip-toe just outside the window, looking in to see papa, and then going off again to play. It was

Never an effort to the Child

to love the father. Dear friends, God can do that for you, and make that His love shall all the day cover you, and that your love shall all the day rise up to Him in deep restfulness and in child-like peace. I am sure God can do it. I am sure God wants to do it, and this is what has brought us together. This is what we need—more love, more love, more of the love of God.

And then look further. What is it we need? Look at our love to those around us, in our daily life, to our family, husband and wife, parents and children, brothers and sisters, masters and servants.

Look at our daily life in business. Look at our daily life in society, with the people whom we meet. Remember the remarks that are so easily made about others. Think of the hasty judgments, of the sharp words, of the thoughtless expressions that escape our lips. Think of how many there are on whom our eyes look and there is no out-going of love towards them. And why is it such an effort to us, and why do we come short? I want you to get hold of one thought, and that is that love is the

Easiest and most Natural thing

in the world—if I have got it in me to love—is the easiest and happiest thing in the world, if I have only got it *in me*. But if I have not got it, then I try and try and do it for a little, and then I fail. Is not God able? I believe He is, and you believe it too. Is not God able to take such possession of the heart of His child? Is not God able, in His mighty power as God, to come into the heart of His child, and to give His love and His Spirit? Is not God able to open a fountain of love, so that in all our intercourse day by day it shall be

Love, Love, Love

flowing out unceasingly? Christ said: "Hereby shall all men know that ye are My disciples, if ye love one another." But oh! the Church of Christ has become a proverb for its contentions and divisions. How terrible! And within the circle of the same little church, of the same little society, of the same little mission, oh, how often between Christians distrust and jealousy; how often unlovingness and harshness!

Oh, friends, do you not feel in your own home and in your own circle and in your business that there is just one thing needed? If my heart was filled with God's love, oh, how easy it would be to live to His glory!

And then there is one thing more. I must not only think of my relation to God and my relation to my fellowmen around me, but I must especially think of my work. Many of us in this hall are workers by whatever name we are called—ministers or missionaries or teachers or helpers.

What is it that is Wanted

in the work of the Church, and why is there so much complaint of want of power and want of success? The one thing that is wanted is the infinite love of God dwelling in us. What would that do for us? It would give us more than one thing. In the first place it would give us a wonderful

Tenderness and Gentleness,

and meekness and humility in dealing with people. My friends, have you ever thought of it?

I have been reading an old book of 150 years ago, and I will tell you what lesson it has taught me. What is the chief mark of Christ Jesus that makes Him so pleasing to the Father? It is His humility. "Learn of Me, for I am meek and lowly in heart." He made His way to the throne of glory in meekness and humility.

Tell me, is not that what is needed in our work? That the spirit of tender compassion and of gentleness should breathe in every utterance about the people whose souls we are seeking—should be the mark of Christ's presence. And then more love would not only

Make us Gentle,

but as with Christ Himself, it would also be the power and the inspiration of a Divine zeal, so that we would sacrifice all.

If we loved others with the love of God, how much more power there would be in our work, how much more sacrifice of time and of ease in praying to God for souls; how much more intercession! Oh! if we loved aright, how much more sacrifice of comfort! how often would we work, as I read of a couple of missionaries in China some years ago, asking: What more can we sacrifice for Jesus?

If the love of God possessed us, how we should sacrifice everything for souls—our formality, our routine, our habits, the ways we have learned to walk, how they would pass away! Not only would we do more work, but different work—work breathed upon by the love of God. And then, when we have got

The Divine Fire,

the divine fire of Christ, the Lamb of God, the Spirit of the Lamb, who gave Himself to the cross, when that is in us, something passes unconsciously and unwittingly out of us on to the people; they do not know what it is, and we do not know; but how many unconverted men would be converted by the power of God's love? Tell me, is not this what every worker needs?

You don't ask me what suggested that subject of perfect love. You feel no one need ask it. It is the one thing the Church needs, and—bless God—it is the one thing He wants to give us. Do let us begin at once. Do not think we are only preparing for to-morrow's blessing, but let us believe that to-night the love can begin to flow.

What are we to Do here?

Suppose we see truly our need in our relation to God, and to society, and to the work we have to do for Christ. "What have we to do?" Well, the first thing we have to do—I think you all know what the answer is—the first thing is, there will have to be the

Discovery and Confession

of sin. We must not only confess our need, that is part of the work, but we must go far deeper, and that is the work that will occupy us to-morrow. I preached on Sunday in preparation for the Convention, and I said to the audience that was here, that, according to our programme, we were going to take the word "perfect love" as a light or lamp from Heaven and to flash it first of all into our own hearts and lives, and look at our lives in the light of that perfect love. That will be to-morrow's work.

And then on Thursday we are going to turn the light of that word "perfect love" on to Christ, to find out what there is in Him and what He is able to do. We are going to look at Christ in the light of that word "perfect love." We are going to find out exactly what Christ can give us, what Christ can do for us, and how we can become possessed of the life and the love shown in Him for us. And then we are going to take

This Search Light

that we have turned upon ourselves first and then upon the face of Jesus, and we are going to turn it upon the face of the world, upon the work we have to do in our own immediate circles and in heathendom, and then in the light of the word of perfect love we are going afresh to work for Jesus.

To-morrow we must begin with ourselves, to let the light

Shine upon Ourselves

and upon our life, And what does that mean? It means that there will have to be within us a distinct discovery of where we fail. I am not going to make out a list of transgressions against the law of love to-night. May God guide the speakers in what they say to-morrow. May God lead them Himself to show what is wrong in our heart and life.

But suppose we have made the discovery of how far we have come short in thought and word and deed of this life of perfect love. What then? Are we to come with these sins to God? Yes, and yet that is not enough. What more is wanted? What we need is this, to find out what is the root of all that. And what is that?

Here I have been a Christian for ten or twenty or thirty years, praying for God to give me love. What is it that is like a devil within me, so that I cannot love? What is it, this temper or this evil spirit? What is this coldness of disposition? And then God will lead us to see what is at the root of all. And what is that? Just one word—

Self! Self! Self!

When God created Adam He gave him self-life; with what object? That Adam should bring that self-life to God to be filled with God's life. And Adam turned away from God and had that self-life closed against God. That is the corruption you and I have inherited from Adam—self. And oh! if grace comes into a Christian and begins to work in his heart and the seed of life is planted amidst the mass of surrounding corruption, how the Christian strives and fights and prays and wrestles to conquer, but in vain. It is self which is the one only cause of his failure. He tries to pluck off a fruit here and a bud there; he cuts off one branch after another of this terrible foe to love. He vows and strives and perhaps does grow a little in love, yet at the bottom has not got rest, and why? There is

Something there that will not Love.

Oh! may God discover to us that terrible something! Self! self! self! We shall then understand that nothing less than death, the death to self, is what must come, if the love of God is to live in us. Thus to come to God, in the confession that there is that in us which must die, and which we cannot slay, is the first step we have to take.

The next thing will be a fresh surrender to God. But oh! I think that with many it must be a different surrender from what they have hitherto made. You know many people honestly surrender themselves to God, but they never understood what it is to surrender self. There is a great difference between surrendering yourselves or surrendering your self, as we use the word self.

Giving up your whole Self

as you are; that root out of which all the evil comes. Many a man says, "Oh! yes, I want to give myself up to God, just as I am, that He may save me," and he has never yet understood what the self is that has to be given up, and what the meaning is of giving it up to God. But God teaches the upright; He teaches him through deep humiliation, and then a man finds out, "I did indeed turn to God, and yet I never turned away from myself. I took myself with my old will and temper, as I was, and gave myself to God; but that was not what God wanted. God wanted me to turn away from self." That is the surrender we must ask God to teach us—to give up

This accursed Self.

Dear friends, do you want to realize perfect love to God in this world? Does that self-will hinder? Oh, you must find out some way of dealing with that self, and you cannot deal with it yourself. It is only the love of God coming in that will cast out self; and before God will do that, self must be brought like a criminal, must be laid at His feet.

Friends, there is no cure for self but death. We must die to self. How can I do that? I cannot kill myself; I cannot be my own executioner. I cannot nail myself to the cross. God alone is the death of self. God Himself must do it. He allowed Christ to die on the Cross, and then when Christ had died God raised Him up. That is why, when God brings a man to see all that there is in Christ and to receive Christ fully, the power of Christ's death can come upon him and he can die to sin; and if he dies to sin, he

Dies to Self.

How can a man be dead to sin if he is not dead to self? Self is the very root of sin. There is no sin if there is no self. Oh! you can take away men's sins, and you can adorn the inner man until you think there is no sin there; but

If Self is there, Sin is there also.

Let us ask God that He may teach us what it is to have self given up. Let us then come and ask God for grace to give up ourselves to Him as we have never done before. Friends, God is love. Will you let Him come in? Will you surrender yourself to God? Yes, that is what we are met to do. There is another thing the surrender to God implies. When you have come and surrendered yourself, you must now keep your place as one actually given into God's hands, in deep resignation, looking to Him for what He will do. Wait upon Him to quicken you and to make you alive from the dead. These are the three things we shall need to do—confession, surrender, and faith. That faith means this: faith in the power of God, who raised Christ from the dead. Yes, friends, the resurrection of Christ is

The Law of the New Life.

Just look at that a moment. Christ Jesus was born in Bethlehem, and just so I am born again by the Holy Spirit. But Christ Jesus had to be born again the second time. He had to live and be tried, tempted and tested, to be developed and to be perfected, and then He had to give up His life, and out of the grave, when He was in hopeless, helpless, dark death, God raised Him up. That is what the Christian must come to. The birth in Bethlehem is the likeness of my new birth when I was converted, but the birth from the grave when Christ became the first-born of the dead is the likeness and promise of that full birth, in which the power of the death and life of Christ come into me, and I know what it is to be dead with Christ and risen with Him—dead unto self and made alive unto God. Oh, friends, we want to set our hearts upon God.

Let the one great thing that you do, from the early morning when you awake to the evening when you go to sleep, be this—

"Have trust in God,"

for what He can do in making you partakers of Christ's death as the death to self, and His life as a life to God and in God, a life in perfect love. Say to God: "My Father, I trust in Thee, for what Thou alone canst do," and say to yourself, "I am going to believe in God, in the mighty power with which He raised Christ from the dead to work in me and in God's children around me."

And now my last question.

"What are we to Expect?"

We know what we are seeking and what we have got to do, but now comes the question, "What are we to expect?" My answer is, "Let us expect something beyond all expectation." Oh! we have so often limited God by our thoughts, and we are doing it still. Yet Paul speaks of "Love that passeth knowledge," and then he further says, "God is able to do above all that we can ask or think." Now prepare yourself for

Something that passeth Knowledge,

for something that is above what you can think, and give God the honour of doing something Divine. Then, further, if you ask me, "What must I expect?" I want to remind you of our last year's motto. There you have it on the wall:

"Jesus Himself."

The work of God the Father is to beget God the Son, and that is the work which goes on through eternity. When we read of the eternal generation, that does not mean that it was a thing in the past. Eternity, what is eternity? Eternity is ever going on. It is an ever-present now, and the one work of God the Father is to beget the Son. What do I expect? I expect God to give all who are prepared the indwelling Christ in their hearts, in a power they have never known, so that we may get rooted and grounded in love, and know the Love that passeth knowledge. That is what we need and what we may expect. God has

Nothing for us but Jesus.

Anything beyond that God cannot give you, but God is willing and able to give this, the living Son born afresh into us. And then He reveals Him to us, and when the living Christ dwells in us, He will break open the fountain of love within us. That is what we want. Expect it now. Fix your eye upon Jesus, Jesus Himself. He must do it. He has done it. He has taught us on Calvary what it is that He gave up His life for, that in His fellowship with us our old man might be crucified with Him. He has done it all for us. We want God to reveal to us what that means, and to make us partakers of it. You may say:

"I have so often tried

to believe in Jesus, but there has been so much failure, and I am so ignorant." Paul prayed that God would strengthen believers mightily by the Holy Spirit. It is only the Father can reveal the Son; and He does it only by the Holy Spirit. The doctrine of the Trinity is to many of us a piece of our orthodoxy, a doctrine we read about in books, occasionally hear of in sermons and confess every Sunday. Oh! listen to that prayer in Ephesians: God the Father giving the Holy Spirit to work mightily in us, and the Holy Spirit making Jesus dwell in us. And when Jesus dwells in us, then we are filled with love unto all the fulness of God—the Triune God, not only in Heaven, but in our hearts. Fix your hearts upon this: the Father must do it, and what the Father will do, I must expect, the Father, God Almighty, to give this Jesus into my heart as an indwelling Saviour; what the Father does is to strengthen us with might by the Holy Spirit in the inner man. Expect that.

Fix your Heart upon God.

This is the one way to the Father, and as we go along step by step in our Convention, let our hearts be filled with this: God is Love. Love is the Divine omnipotence. Love is the life and the glory of God. Yes. God is Love. There is the love of the Father, and the love of the Son, and the love of the Spirit. Let us fix our hope on the love of the Father giving the Son into our hearts. Let us rejoice in the Son coming with God's perfect love to dwell within. Let us bow in stillness while the Holy Spirit works mightily within us to shed abroad the love. God will come unto us, and will bring us into His banqueting-house, and His banner over us will be love. May God teach every waiting heart to expect this, nothing less than the Perfect Love of God perfected in us. God grant it.

THE CLOSING ADDRESS

THE words from which I wish to speak to you this evening, and which I want you to take away with you as our farewell, you will find in the 17th chapter of the Gospel according to St. John, the last verse. They are among the farewell words of our Lord Jesus as He went out to Gethsemane. The last part of the verse reads as follows: "That the love wherewith Thou hast loved Me may be in them and I in them."

Perfect love has been the subject of our meditation during this Convention. Perfect love has been our prayer and our song and our constant plea. Perfect love is the promise for the fulfilment of which we wait. I cannot speak of anything else this evening; perhaps cannot do better than try and gather up the lessons and the thoughts of the past three days, so as to help you, as we part, to go away in the spirit of strong and loving faith in the love of God and of what He is going to do for us; to go away as those who are utterly and entirely given up to love; who are to let perfect love rule within their heart and will; who are to be so utterly given up to the perfect love of God, that He may be glorified in all our life.

May the everlasting love that came from heaven to die and suffer and wrestle for our souls; may the everlasting love that can wrestle through the feebleness of human words to win souls entirely to Himself, come amongst us and take possession and make us wholly God's!

I want to speak to you of perfect love in the light which this text throws upon it. And the first thought that I find here is this: If I want to find out the nature of perfect love, I must look up to

God's Love to Christ.

That is the first thought. The text says: "Father, that the love wherewith Thou hast loved Me may be in them." This is Christ's conclusion of His whole prayer. It is the whole object of His work, and that object is this: That the love that I have tasted, that the love which rested on Me, and dwells in Me, may now pass on to them. And so, if you want to know what the life of perfect love is, you must rise up to heaven itself and see what the love of God to Christ is.

And if you ask: How can I know what this perfect love in the Godhead is? I can only answer, The Father gave His own life to the Son; the Son was begotten of the Father, out of His bosom; in the depths of the Godhead Christ came forth from the Father. If God had not been love; if God had been anything that we could call selfish, He would have been content to be God alone. But He would not be alone. From eternity He set His Son before Him as His image and His glory. He gave birth to the Son. When a man gives out his own life to another, that is love; and the love of God is that He gave all His life to His only-begotten Son, and He said that, to all eternity, He never would live without His Son.

Here I learn the first lesson this evening, that love means this—a birth out of the heart of God. That is

The only True Love

upon earth. Love that will live and last through eternity. Even now still it can only come out of the Godhead. It is the work of God to give that birth; and, dear friends, as really as Jesus Christ was born of God, and in the resurrection was perfected as the first begotten from the dead, you must be born of God, in the power of the resurrection, or you have no share in the love of God or the heaven of God.

Let us remember that. If we have been trying to learn the lesson, I think God will teach us more and more that love means giving; and giving all. We sometimes give a little, but not all. To give all—that is love! What did the Father do to the Son? He made Him heir of all things. The Father let Christ share in everything. God gave Him a seat in His Throne; He gave Him a place in the worship of the angels; by Him He created the world; He gave Him all His glory and all His love.

Do you want to know what love is? Oh, my heart cannot take it in, nor my tongue express it; my thoughts cannot reach to all its fulness. Love means—giving all! It is that with God, and it is that with us too. If you are to have love, it means you are to give up everything to God; everything. God cannot be limited. With God love means giving His life to His Son, and with that giving everything! That is the love of God to Christ.

Another thought. How did God prove His love for Christ? He gave Him His own life; He gave Him all things throughout the universe; and then sent Him to die! You say, That is strange; is that the love of God? Yes.

Oh, you say, that was an exceptional thing, which became necessary, but did not belong to the essence of God's love. No, indeed; this sending His Son to die is the highest and most wondrous part of God's love to Christ. And how does it prove the love of God? I will tell you. It was not possible in the nature of things that God should come to die upon earth for sinners; but God put

This Honour upon His Son

when He said: "Go and become a man, and in love live the life of man and of humanity." It was the infinite love of the Father to the Son which made Him say, I will put this honour upon my Son. God in His love sent Christ to die. We have heard that, in different ways, love always means death; the death of self; and God sent Christ and said: "Go and obey My Word, and then lay down Thy life to die to sin and the world and self; give up Thy life entirely for Me and My glory."

My friends, as you think of the love of God, has it ever said to you that you must die? The highest point of God's love is that He invites us to die utterly to self, to be like Himself and His Son, perfect in love. God's love to Christ means death. May we have grace to say: I would enter into the death of Jesus, I would be nothing in myself, O my God! May Thy love consent to accept of me to be nothing.

And then God raised Him from the dead: that also was the love of God, which led Christ in the path of death to the resurrection life, the resurrection glory, the eternal glory of heaven. If you want to learn the nature of love, remember

These Three Things:

that love gave birth to the Son, that love gave all to the Son; and then love claimed all from the Son. Oh, if we are to know perfect love, do not let us think this is too high for simple people. Do not let us say

We cannot be Troubled

with theological doctrines about the relation of the Father to the Son. If we are to spend eternity with God, in the fellowship with the Father and the Son, there is surely nothing of such absorbing interest for us as to know what the relation of the Father and the Son, what God's love to Christ is. God gave His Son to me and with Him gave all; and now, love is—God claiming everything. Only as I die can I enter into the new, the resurrection life, into perfect love, into the glory of God.

There is a second thought in this passage. I must not only look at the love of the Father to Christ, but I must look at

The Love of Christ to us.

How do I get that from this text? Very simply. Jesus prays, "Father, that the love wherewith Thou hast loved Me may be in them." What does that imply? Christ wants to share the love God gave to Him with us; and He goes to the Father and says, "Father, here are those whom I have redeemed. Father, I plead that they may have all the love that Thou hast given Me, and that it may rest in them." Is not that Christ's wonderful love? The Father took Christ up into a perfect likeness with Himself. As He had given all to the Son in the depth of Godhead, He allowed the Son to show on earth what love is by giving back all to the Father. And Christ wants us to grow up into a perfect likeness with Himself. As God gave all He had to Christ, so Christ gives all He has to us, even to the love of the Father. It is the love of Christ that prays to the Father for us, that the Father's love may come into us.

What does that Teach Us?

It reminds us of what Christ is doing in Heaven. Christ as a Mighty King on the Throne of God prays day and night for us. He gives up His life in glory to pray for us. He cannot die a second time, but just as He died on the Cross on earth, He gives up His life in Heaven to prayer that the love of God may come down upon us. Oh, friends, that is what love does.

You tell me you want to know what love will do.

Love will Pray for others.

It will say, just like Christ, "I have got this wonderful blessing of God's love, and I will give it to those around me." It should be the prayer of us all, "Oh, let the love of God come down upon them also!" There is nothing that should make Christians so ashamed as their non-appreciation of the influence of intercession for others.

How many Christians who have

Thought Everything was Right

with them; who spend their little time in prayer daily, their quarter-hour or half-hour and get benefit from it; and yet have never made it a rule to make time for prayer for others? Have you ever set your heart upon the thought, "I can by much prayer bring down a blessing from heaven upon some one else"?

Love calls on God. It comes to God as the fountain of love, and has got something to say. It gives its time and its ardent heart's desire and says, "Father, Oh, for a blessing on those around me." Friends, Jesus the King spends all His time in heaven praying.

Do you Believe it?

It is true. And how much time do you spend in this loving exercise? How little of this love we have! Father, forgive us. If you want to know what love is, look at the love of Christ praying for us.

And then, just think further of what Jesus said in the rest of that prayer, of how He spoke of what He had done for those disciples: "I have given them Thy Word"; and in the words that precede our text He says, "I have declared Thy Name unto them."

Love not only prays;

Love Works.

Christ had been working for three years upon those disciples. How patiently He had borne with them! How marvellously He had instructed them and led them step by step, humbling Himself to their weak capacities!

Love not only prays, but it teaches, it watches and it labours. Oh, we have been talking about perfect love, and we want to be perfected in love. Remember that, if we study it in the light of Christ's love, it means that we give up ourselves to pray for others and to work for others.

And then one thing more. Christ not only prays and works, but He dies. He says in this chapter, "I sanctify Myself; I give Myself as a sacrifice for them that they may be sanctified."

Love Dies for those it Loves.

You remember those solemn words in 1 John 3:16: "We ought to lay down our lives for the brethren." There ought to be such love in us, that we so give our lives for the brethren that, when it became needful, dying for them would be the natural result of our love. Love not only prays; love labours. Love not only labours; love dies. God's love is seen in that He gave Christ up to the death as an honour and a privilege. Christ's love was seen in that He gave His life. Perfect love gives its life for others. It is true in God, in Christ, in ourselves.

The third thought to which our text leads us is

The Conditions

on which this perfect love can be ours. For whom does Christ pray in this prayer? "That the love wherewith Thou hast loved Me may be *in them*, and I *in them*." Is that for the whole world? No. For whom, then?

He gave certain marks of those for whom He asked that God's love should be in them, and I want you to attend to those marks very specially. These marks indicate the conditions that are required if we are to receive this blessing of the perfect love of God in our hearts. What are these marks? The first mark is this—"They are not of the world as I am not of the world." Separation out of the midst of the world.

Oh, Christians, if you want to know what perfect love is, you must come out of the world;

You must be Separate.

You tell me, "I do not understand what that means." Never mind. Say to God, "Lord, I want to come out of the world; I want to live like a man who is not of this world, but of the other world." The love of God cannot dwell in your heart if the spirit of the world is there. It is impossible. It is only when we go out from the world that the love of God can enter into and take possession.

Another mark. Christ says, "I have given them Thy Word and they have received it, and they have believed that Thou hast sent Me." That is another mark—

Receiving the Word in Obedience

and faith. They forsook all to follow Christ; and they received His word and testimony, set their whole confidence upon it, and that is what St. John sets before us as the mark of perfect love. "Whoso keepeth His Word, in him verily is the love of God perfected."

Let me say this for your comfort: the love and the faith of these disciples for whom Christ prayed was very defective, and yet Christ accepted it as the obedience and the faith of loving hearts. And so we can be sure, that if we come to Christ with our feeble beginnings, that He will receive our love, and will day by day lead us in the path of perfect love and perfect obedience— not the obedience of angels, but the perfect obedience of faith. That is the second condition of love. The first condition is separation from the world, the second obedience to His Word, and the third condition is

Unity with Believers around us.

Christ prays for that: "Father, that they may be one." God's children must acknowledge each other, wherever they meet, however they may differ in their church organizations or in other things. My brother must be as dear to me as Christ Jesus is. *God's children must draw close together, or the gift of perfect love cannot come.* In the fellowship of love they must prove to the world that there is something in them that is different from the world, that the Spirit of God and of Heaven, of Perfect Love, is in them. Dr. Saphir has somewhere said, that in the Primitive Church there were many differences, but that as long as they looked more on the things on which they agreed than those on which they differed, the unity of love was maintained unbroken.

If the Church of Christ had only done that, how different would be our state to-day! But we have been looking too much on the things on which we differ, though many of these things are comparatively of little importance. Do let us get hold of the thought that, just as we must be separate from the world, and joined to Christ in obedience to His Word, so we must also be joined to each other.

My love to my brother is the sure,

The Only Real Test

of my love to God and to Jesus. If we are to seek and to find the life of Perfect Love, if God's love to Christ is to be in us, as He prays, and He in us, the condition must be fulfilled—we must give up ourselves to see that all our intercourse with God's children is love—unselfish, tender, self-sacrificing, ministering love.

But lest any be discouraged by the fear that these conditions of the path to perfect love are beyond their reach, let me remind them of one thing.

In Holy Scripture we find a great deal about two stages in the Christian life—the Old Testament and the New; a time of preparation and a time of fulfilment. The longer I study God's Word and the Christian life, the deeper my conviction grows that the difference between the Old and New Testaments is a radical one, and runs not only through the life of the Church, but through the life of every believer.

Now it is for His disciples Christ is praying, as He asks, "Father, that the love wherewith Thou hast loved Me may be in them and I in them." It would seem this was

Something that had not Come yet.

They did indeed love Jesus, but their love was an elementary, a feeble love, the love of beginners. Christ had said, "If ye love Me, keep My commands." No doubt they went away from that sacred hour with full purpose to keep His Word, and yet how soon they forsook their Master! Christ saw that they did indeed love Him and longed to obey Him; He Himself said, "The spirit is willing, but the flesh is weak." Christ saw their loving obedience, but they were still only in the preparatory stage, and their best efforts were but feeble. "To will, is present with me, but how to perform that which is good, I find not": this was their experience. And yet they were in the sure path to perfect love.

Christ was Training them

for something better: amid all their failure He saw their heart was right with Him. Thank God for the comfort that can give us.

There is another stage; it is this that Christ prays for. He seems to say, "Father, there is a new time coming, when Thou shalt pour down Thy Holy Spirit upon them; when the love of God shall fill them as it fills Me; when Thy love in which I live shall be in them as in Me, and I in them." Christ was praying for the Day of Pentecost; the three conditions, without which the Day of Pentecost could not come, were found in them. And the Day of Pentecost came, and God's love filled them. Our heart may be saying honestly: "Perfect love, yes, perfect love. This my constant plea," and yet we feel we have not attained to it.

Let us Hold on

in the spirit to these three things—separation from the world, from its spirit, and from its pleasures; acceptance of God's Word in faith and obedience; unity with all God's children,—and Christ, Who led His disciples on so wonderfully, will lead us on too.

We now come to the fourth thought that our text suggests. The

Love of God Perfected in us.

This is what Christ prays for: "Father, that the love wherewith Thou hast loved Me may be in them and I in them." I said this refers to the Day of Pentecost. In St. John 14:20 Christ says, "*At that day* ye shall know that I am in My Father, and I in you." He also said, "If ye love Me, keep My commandments, and the Father will love you." There was a love to Christ which was already in them. There was also a love which they were still to get through the Holy Spirit. This they obtained at Pentecost, and this we must have if we would know perfect love. And the question comes to us, What does it mean to have the love of the Father in us—the love wherewith the Father loved His Son? What does that mean? What does God aim to accomplish in us? "That the love wherewith Thou hast loved Me may be in them." First of all I must understand that the love of God is going to be within me. How is the love of God, possessing and ruling and filling my inmost being, to be in me? Just as thinking and feeling and willing is in me, and it is most easy and natural for me to think and feel and will, even so when the love of God really fills my heart, love will flow out spontaneously and continuously. Instead of it being a duty, as it is in the earlier disciple stage, with its effort and failure, it becomes a delight, and there is a love that cannot help loving, because God's love has been shed abroad and has taken complete possession. Up to this time there has been an inward life of self continually getting the mastery. The love of self and of sin has been very deep in me. What Christ's prayer asks and promises is, that we are now to have an inward life of love;

In the place of Sin and Self

the love of God to Christ is now to fill the heart. Instead of having to try to love always, and so often failing, love comes in as an indwelling Divine power constituting the very life of the soul, and loves spontaneously, continuously, and most joyfully. Love has filled the heart. Think of this. My heart, my heart, MY heart becomes the habitation of the holy love of God to Jesus in its Divine joy and blessedness, its infinite power, its everlasting glory! "That the love wherewith Thou hast loved Me may be in them"! That love is to be *in us*, our second nature, our new self, our very selves.

And then, note further, this love is to come through the Holy Spirit. Yes; the work of the Holy Spirit is this: that in and through Him the Father begets the Son. He is the love which is their living bond of union. You know it is a doctrine of the Church that the Spirit proceeds from the Father and the Son; and therefore, when Christ met the Father in the glory after His resurrection, the Holy Spirit began to flow; and the Father gave the Spirit to the Son, and the Spirit flowed down from the Father through the Son to the disciples. And it is to this Holy Spirit we are now to look to bring the love of God as a heavenly reality, as a Divine life, into our hearts. We have the Holy Spirit. So the disciples had the Holy Spirit also before the Day of Pentecost, but only as a secret power working in them. They did not know Him as a Person. They had Him given to live within them, but they did not know Him. They could not indeed yet know Him, as bringing the very love of Christ to them from the throne of God in the glory. And just so there are the

Two Stages

in our experience. We may struggle and wrestle, and try and fight for love, but we don't succeed. But the words of our text give us the precious promise which gives us hope. As the Son prays to the Father, "That the love wherewith Thou hast loved Me may be in them," so we receive the blessed assurance that our hearts can be filled with the love of God in a way and to an extent that we have never known before, in the power of the Holy Ghost.

Once more. If you want to know how this love of God is to be perfected, it is not only that you have to give the whole heart, and wait for the Holy Spirit of God; but, above all things, you have to look to Jesus, through whom the Spirit comes and whom the Spirit will reveal! Look how Christ connects the two things: "That *Thy love* may be *in them* and *I in them*." The indwelling love of God and the indwelling Son of God are

Inseparable.

You cannot understand it, but the Son of God is the love of God. He was born of God's love; He was sent by God's love; He was raised from the dead by God's love; and He dwells in the glory in God's love. And therefore while we look for the Holy Spirit, let us set our hearts wide open, and know that we can have within a holy temple that can be filled with love, because Christ, who holds within Himself all God's love, comes to dwell there. Let us expect this with a trust and a confidence and a clinging to Christ, "In Whom the love of God is manifested." And as the prayer of Jesus brought Pentecost to the early disciples, so the prayer of Jesus brings Pentecost to the individual soul now. It is the intercession of Christ which can bring Pentecost, and perfect the love of God in the heart of each one of us.

I feel that I have but stammered with great feebleness in speaking of these things. Just let me ask, in conclusion, what is needed now that we who are gathered here may enter into the possession of this love? How can we go away to-morrow, after all the teaching, all the praying, all the singing, with all the thoughts of the last few days gathered up into one thought? Let me ask you

Two Simple Questions.

Do you believe that this prayer can be fulfilled in you? Do you believe that it is God's will that the Holy Spirit should reveal His love to Jesus as a living reality and a continuous experience within your heart? I believe it! I believe it is God's will for you and for me. Perfect love is the love that is in

God; that is in Christ; that is in the Holy Spirit for us, that He may bring it into our hearts. The fruit of the Spirit is love. Oh, look at the mystery of the love of the Father to Christ His Son, the love that fills eternity. Look at the love of the Son to us—heavenly love made manifest on earth. The love that the Spirit brings is this very same Divine and heavenly love; and this perfect, Divine love, the Holy Spirit will pour out in our hearts. Let us fix our faith upon this. There is a perfect love for me, and the Holy Spirit is the messenger to come and bring it through Jesus and from Jesus to me. Nothing short of this can satisfy the longing soul; and I want it in my heart; I may count upon it. Why? Because Jesus prayed the Father that it should come. Have you set your heart upon that, and

Do you Believe

God means that it can come? The love wherewith the Father loved the Son is a Divine supernatural reality, as a heavenly power to dwell in and have possession of you.

Come, my brother, let us listen for a moment to the voice of Christ—"Father, Thou lovest Me, and I love them; according to the riches of Thy glory grant that the love wherewith Thou hast loved Me may enter the hearts of My disciples, and dwell there always, so that I can dwell there." Let us say, "Father, I believe it can be done!"

And then my second question: If you believe it can be done,

Are you going to Yield

yourself to it? Love claims all. Love is very exacting. God asked Christ to give His life up to Him, and He could not do anything else; and Christ asks of His disciples that they should forsake all for Him; Christ asks that we should be ready to give up our life for the brethren. Perfect love wants a perfect heart, perfectly given up to love alone. It asks that we should yield ourselves and say, "Lord, here I am; and I part with everything in the world that love may have possession of every word I speak, and every thought I have, and every act I do; that every moment of my life may be a sacrifice to Thy love, so that nothing but love can come out of me!" Are you afraid to speak thus? Do you feel as if you did not dare to pray thus, because you know not how it can come? It must come as a Divine supernatural gift, as the power of God. It is not a thing which can be attained, or reached, or grasped. But are you willing to surrender yourself to be like Christ—nothing but a servant of Divine love? Oh, my friends, it is a very solemn thing that our love for God on the Day of Judgment is going to be tried by our love for man and our treatment of our fellow-man. We have to be judged by the test of love. Do remember that. You are not going to win a crown of glory by faith without works, but by faith and works of love. You get pardon by faith without one good work, but in the Day of Judgment good deeds are to be taken into account. Remember every day as you come to God that

God Judges

of your love to Him by your conduct to your fellow-men. What do we read in John? "Let us not love in word, but in deed and in truth, and we shall assure our hearts before God." "He that loveth not his brother whom he hath seen, how can he love God Whom he hath not seen?" Your love for God is an imagination, a sentiment, a delusion, if your heart is not full of love for your fellow-man.

Oh, friends, this perfect love comes as a very solemn claim, with its demand on every moment of my life that the world around may see that it is real. Are you willing to give up your life to it? I am not going to ask at this moment if you have attained to it; but, are you willing to submit to God that the love with which God loved Christ, the love that sent Him to die for men, may have you wholly for itself? God wants every brother and every sister in this room to say, "My God, I give myself up to live only, and always, and wholly for the love of God." You feel it is impossible; you feel utterly helpless; you cannot undertake to live this life of perfect love. Fear not,

The more Helpless the Better.

We need to sink right down into despair. It was after Christ was dead!—dead!—dead, and in the grave, that God raised Him up to the glory; and you must sink down into death and utter helplessness and say, "My God, I want love, and my love is passing away from me; O be Thou my support!" You must sink down into

The Grave of your own Impotence,

the grave of self, and let God Himself lift you up! If you are only willing to acknowledge God's claim, and to say, "My Father, here I am. This love, wherewith Thou didst love Thy Son, it is too high for me—beyond my reach. But if Thou wilt hear His prayer, here I am, let that love enter and take possession. I yield myself to its blessed power—let it live in me!"

Will you claim this? Will you accept this? I know it is not an easy thing. You think, perhaps, you are not now prepared for it; but come, come now, this evening. God grant that each one of us may now give our answer to these questions: Do I really believe there is such a thing as the words of this prayer being fulfilled in my spirit? Is it possible? Can you say your "Yea and Amen, O my God"? And then

"Am I Willing

to surrender absolutely my whole life, day by day to wait upon God for the power and love of God to maintain within me the life of perfect love, of God's love to Christ living in me?"

And then the last question. We are now about to unite in an act of consecration: Am I ready now in faith to believe in the mighty power of the Holy Spirit to bring the full answer to the prayer, "That the love wherewith Thou hast loved me may be in them, and I in them"? Am I ready to believe that God will grant to me what is written in His Word, "Love perfected in us; we perfected in love"? God holds out the promise. The mighty, all-prevailing intercession of Christ pleads for it. The Holy Spirit can and will work it. The Three-One God is my surety for it. Lord! I do believe; grant it for Thy Name's sake. Amen.

www.ingramcontent.com/pod-product-compliance
Lightning Source LLC
Chambersburg PA
CBHW071802020426
42331CB00008B/2381